DIARY OF DAILY PRAYER
Second Edition

DIARY OF DAILY PRAYER
Second Edition

∽∾∽

J. Barrie Shepherd

Westminster John Knox Press
LOUISVILLE • LONDON

Scripture quotations unless otherwise noted are from the Revised Standard Version of the Bible, copyright © 1946, 1952, 1971, and 1973 by the Division of Christian Education of the National Council of the Churches of Christ in the U.S.A., and are used by permission.

Book design by Sharon Adams
Cover design by Pam Poll Graphic Design

Published by Westminster John Knox Press
Louisville, Kentucky

This book is printed on acid-free paper that meets the American National Standards Institute Z39.48 standard. ♾

PRINTED IN THE UNITED STATES OF AMERICA

02 03 04 05 06 07 08 09 10 11 — 10 9 8 7 6 5 4 3 2 1

Library of Congress Cataloging-in-Publication Data

Shepherd, J. Barrie.
    Diary of daily prayer / J. Barrie Shepherd.— 2nd ed.
      p. cm.
    ISBN 0-664-22565-9
    1. Prayers. I. Title.

BV245 .S5 2002
242'.2—dc21

2001040850

I dedicate this book to the five women in my life:
Mhairi, my wife, and Alison, Fiona, Nicola, and Catriona,
my four daughters. I do so in gratitude for many things,
but especially for a growing sensitivity
to the subtly powerful ways in which the language we use
excludes the feminine experience, the female world.
In this book I have tried to avoid the all-too-typical use
of specific male words as generic terms to cover both sexes.
At times I have failed. In other places I leave unresolved questions,
such as my repeated use of "Father" as the most intimate address
for God. I have tried. I leave it to others to further the attempt.
And I am grateful to all those who inspired it in my life.

CONTENTS

PREFACE TO SECOND EDITION

Some twenty-five years ago and more, this little book first saw the light of day. Its official publication date was to be in early 1975, but one of the very first printed copies was rushed to me—"hot off the press"—in mid-December 1974, so that it could be home in Scotland, in my parents' hands, in time for Christmas. My parents are now both long gone, but that memory revives in me a deep sense of gratitude for their loving nurture, and for all they did that encouraged in me whatever gifts I may have received.

As happens with almost all books—including many of my own—the time came when *Diary of Daily Prayer* went out of print, and before long even the few copies I held in my personal stock were exhausted. Yet at speaking engagements, teaching assignments, General Assemblies, and other such gatherings of the faithful across the intervening years, I received continuing requests for copies of the book, and/or inquiries about where copies might be obtained. So many people have spoken and written to me about their own use of the blank pages provided to form their personal prayer diaries and journals. Some have even sent me samplings from those pages. From time to time I have also been surprised, usually in worship settings, to hear someone reading excerpts from the book, and have been astonished at its continuing vitality and its ability to address the here and now with both insight and grace. (I hesitate, naturally, to apply such words to my own writing, and do so only in the firm conviction that all is, and has been, a gift—a gift generously given, and freely to be shared.)

In view of all this I was both honored, and delighted, when Westminster John Knox Press expressed interest in presenting a Twenty-Fifth Anniversary Edition of this, my first published work. Even though the publication date has now lagged a little beyond the actual anniversary, I still rejoice in the lives that have been touched and blessed over the years by the words and thoughts set down here, and in this opportunity to extend that ministry over the next few years. My prayer is now, as it was back then, that these words of mine may clear the way for silence, that deepest silence into which the living Word may speak yet again, and speaking create light in darkness, new life from dusty death.

ABOUT THIS BOOK

As an undergraduate at The University of Edinburgh, I managed to attend a graduate-level seminar at New College. The topic was "Prayer," and the instructor, the late John Baillie. As the bell rang, a dry, wrinkled stick of a man in a teaching robe slowly entered the room. He approached the podium, cleared his throat, and proceeded to address the class in a voice as young and vibrant as a June morning in the Scottish Highlands. I do not recall much of what he said but, for me, Baillie embodied the very spirituality we had come to learn about. I learned that prayer is not greatly concerned with words; it is a matter of life lived in the presence of the Lord.

This volume is arranged in the form of a diary, somewhat along the lines of John Baillie's classic little book, *Diary of Private Prayer.* It goes without saying that Baillie's work will never be replaced, or superseded. However, if my book can supplement what he achieved, or, better still, continue his attempt to provide a series of launching points for the essentially private, essentially personal event of prayer, I will be more than satisfied. It is to that purpose that space has been provided each day for the addition of individual petitions, intercessions, confessions, and exclamations of praise. This is not only my diary. If used to the full, it becomes a truly personal Diary of Prayer for each reader.

The reader may notice that many of the prayers contain more implicit than fully explicit references to Jesus, the Christ. This characteristic springs from a conviction that the traditional formula of ending every prayer with a specific reference to Christ—as if by affixing such a seal one assures a speedy and favorable hearing from the Lord—is not necessary, and may even encourage the loose and empty use of the name of our Lord. It also expresses my belief that God hears the earnest prayers of all persons, whether or not they name the name of Christ in every prayer. Where such explicit references are appropriate to the content of the prayer, they are made. However, just as much of Jesus' own claim about himself was made, not directly, in explicit proclamation of his divine status, but indirectly, through the parables, rhetorical questions, symbolic actions, and eloquent silences of his life and ministry, just so is he present in these prayers—quietly, gently, often unnamed, but always there, at the heart.

One final word: These prayers are designed to form a dialogue. Silence should have a part in every one of them—the waiting silence that listens for the Word of the Lord. Rather than try to predetermine the place of silence in each prayer, I have left it to the discretion of the reader. All I ask is that my book may claim a space for listening as well as for speaking, for waiting upon the Lord, as well as for calling upon his name.

DIARY OF DAILY PRAYER
Second Edition

DAY ONE

Miracles

In an age of miracles, O God,
when the horizons of the planets
are displayed in our morning newspapers,
and folk take routine walks in the vacuum of space,
in an age of miracles,
I come to you in search of a miracle.

I come because,
despite its spectacular achievements,
this is also the age of anxiety.
And I am deeply anxious.

I come because,
despite the mind-expanding times in which I live,
these are also times of confusion, loneliness,
and the loss of meaning.
And I am profoundly confused.

In these quiet morning moments, Lord,
speak to me of your own miracle,
the miracle of love.
Perform, here and now, within me
the miracle of forgiveness, of renewal,
of life out of death.
Set before my eyes
the entire miraculous spectrum of your creation,
the infinite majesty of your universe,
the fathomless mystery of your atom,
the boundless possibility of the human spirit.

Then send me forth this day,
to bear these miracles to the heart
of an otherwise spectacularly empty world.

DAY ONE

Relaxing

Father, so often I fail
to find you in my praying,
despite all my best efforts.
I enter grimly into prayer,
trying to gather up all my wandering thoughts
and suppress them, control them for you.
I seek your presence, Lord,
attempting to clear my mind of all possible distractions,
all conceivable interruptions.
Yet, no matter how I concentrate,
my thoughts thread their way back
to the business of my daily life and work.
Am I so wrong in this, Lord?
Surely if these are the things that concern me,
the matters around which my life revolves,
then they should form the content of my prayers.
When will I learn that prayers
are not time set aside from life,
reserved for thinking pure and holy thoughts,
but prayer is a lifelong dialogue with you
concerning all that is important in my life?

Help me, now,
not to concentrate,
but rather to relax.
Convince me that I cannot raise myself
into your holy presence by sheer determination,
that you are always already here,
and all I have to do
is to open myself to your presence.
Help me
to be myself
in my praying, Lord.

DAY TWO

Your tolerance

For this new day of promise and possibility, Lord,
I want to praise you not only with my lips,
but with my living.

Teach me to share this day with others
in a true spirit of celebration, openness, and grace.
In every hour preserve me
from the smooth and easy answers of intolerance.
Deny to me, Father, the idle luxury
of venting my frustrations and rage
upon the usual, carefully selected scapegoats.
Help me to recognize within my own heart
all the potential for racism and bigotry,
for blind violence, brutality, and repression,
that I am so swift to point out in others.
And let me see that this inner potential finds
its most immediate, and perhaps its most destructive
expression in the scorn and contempt I reserve
for those who dare to disagree with me.
Teach me to value all with whom I spend my time
as fellow human beings,
your precious gifts to me this day.
Fill me with *your* tolerance—
no empty, undiscriminating acceptance of everything,
rather a difficult, testing tolerance,
a tolerance that combines
a basic, non-negotiable respect for all individuals
with a self-sacrificing quest for justice and truth.

Above all, Father, fill me with the one power
that can bring people together by attraction,
and not by compulsion—the power of your love.
In that power may I spend my self
in healing, in reconciling,
in binding up this splintered world.

DAY TWO

Honest gratitude

Gratitude is a difficult emotion, Father.
So often I am told to thank you
for food and clothing, health and strength,
the beauty of nature, the privilege of freedom,
but I don't really feel grateful.
I go through the motions of thanks, nothing more.

Yet, when I consider,
there *are* many things for which I am thankful.
I thank you, Lord,
for moments of inspiration,
flashes of joy, glimpses of truth.
I thank you for the hidden strengths
that carry me through the stresses of each hour.
I thank you for peace and relaxation
at the close of a hard day's work,
for grace that surprises me, now and then,
in the midst of living, and transforms it for an instant,
for the comfort, and frankness, and joy
of a few real friends.
I am grateful too, Lord.
that you have not abandoned me
to my own vanity, conceit, and prejudice,
but have kept nagging away at the back of my mind
with hard choices, testing decisions,
the constant challenge, in all that I do,
to find my life in losing it.

Most of all I thank you for Jesus Christ,
who opened himself to the utmost
that I might see true life in him,
fully lived out, and fully died out.
For his life risen and living in me this night,
I thank you, Father, and rejoice.

DAY THREE

My body

Sometimes when I awaken,
it is as if I am returning to my body, Lord.
What is this thing that I call "my body"?
Is it something that I own, Father,
like "my house," or "my car"?
Could it be something I relate to,
like "my wife," "my child," "my parents"?
Do I *own* my body? Or *am* I my body?
Is it I who demand daily food and shelter,
comfort, tenderness, sexual expression,
recreation, rest, and relaxation?
Or is it "only my body" that needs such things?
Is my body flabby and in need of discipline,
or am I?
Who gets sick, my body, or myself?
And just who is growing old at such a speed?
Yes, Lord, at times, language makes things
much more difficult to comprehend.

Teach me, Father, to know myself
as a unity of both body and spirit.
Help me to grow into a fuller self-awareness,
an awareness in which I recognize myself as a person,
a person who is a body,
a body who is more than flesh and bone and blood.

Help me to accept the mystery of my own self,
a body formed by your hands, enlivened by your breath.
And thus may I accept my body,
all its strengths, all its flaws.
May I be my body,
and in so doing be also your creation,
the living being you molded me to be,
the new creation that you shaped with your own
flesh and blood in Jesus Christ, my Lord.

DAY THREE

Friends

Friends were with me today, Lord,
people I love,
and who love me,
people I trust,
and who trust me,
people I enjoy being with,
no matter where, or how, or why.
Friends were with me today.

I thank you for my friends
and for all they bring to my living.
For the way they give of themselves to me,
for the way they help me give of myself,
and even be myself, and more than myself,
I give you my deepest thanks, Father.
I thank you, Lord, for the simple
but real kinds of support,
and comfort, and strength I can draw
from my friends.

But most of all I thank you
for the ways in which you reveal yourself
to me through friendship,
for all of the moments in which,
through frail but wonderful human instruments,
you sing to me of grace and mercy,
of the risk of commitment
and the challenge of response,
of the strong, sure knowledge of acceptance
in the heart of a true friend,
in the heart of a true father,
in your heart, my God and my Redeemer.

Grant me now a restful night,
the grace to rise refreshed tomorrow,
and the faith to be a friend to all I meet.

DAY FOUR

Journey

Another day begins, Lord,
another journey—dawn to dusk—
in the voyage of discovery we call "life."
As I set out, I pause to ask your blessing,
your guidance along the way,
your welcome when I reach my destination.

Grant me this day
the smile of a song upon my lips,
the lilt of lively companionship along the road,
the wisdom to see the way ahead and hold to it,
the strength and courage to overcome all obstacles,
and the openness to share these gifts
with all whose way is tangled and obscure.

Do not permit me, Father,
to wander from the route,
mazing myself in the circling paths of selfishness,
straying with the pride
that always seems to dog my footsteps.
But also, Lord, do not allow me
to travel with such intense concentration on the goal
that I cannot take the time
to enjoy the wonders along the way,
the tiny, everyday marvels that call on me
to stop a while, and celebrate,
and praise you for the journey
as well as for the destination.

And when I reach the journey's end,
grant me safe lodging,
loved ones to greet me,
and a place to rest and be with you again.

DAY FOUR

Noontime and evening

In the calm, relaxed quietness
of this evening hour
you are telling me something, Lord,
something about the frenzy,
the hectic, panicked pace
of life at noonday.

For, despite all the crises,
all the impossible demands,
the unmeetable assignments,
the inhuman deadlines
of the heat of the day,
somehow, evening always comes,
the tempo slows down,
and those decisions at noon
can be reviewed
in the cool, clear light
of eternity.

Let the peace of evening become
so much a part of me,
and me a part of it, Lord,
that I can take it with me
into the working day tomorrow.
Let me store this peace away, now,
at the back of my mind,
the roots of my soul,
and then bring it out,
even momentarily,
when all seems lost and hopeless.

Thus grant me, Father,
to share a little here and now,
in the vision,
the experience, of eternity.

DAY FIVE

For peace

I awaken to the early morning peace,
and I praise you, Lord, for the promise of the morning.
In this new day
let my desire for peace
become something more than
a fond hope, a plaintive song,
an emotional high, a political slogan,
a patch on my blue jeans.
Let the reality of peace,
all of its rich connotations—
wholeness and concern,
cooperation, selflessness, communion—
take root and grow within me.

May I take peace behind the wheel of my automobile,
peace into the supermarket,
discount store, and coffee shop.
May peace be with me in my workplace,
setting the boundaries, determining the textures
of all my words and actions.
As I break bread with my family and friends,
may that bread become a sacrament of peace.
If I should differ and dispute with those around me,
may I differ within the overarching context
of that basic regard for the dignity of all your children
which is at the heart of all true peace, Lord.

So let this active,
all-encompassing power of peace
become the source and the goal of all of my living.
And thus, may I know something
of that peculiar blessedness you have promised
to all true peacemakers
through the Prince of Peace.

DAY FIVE

Time-out

Eternal and ever-living God,
I come before you this evening
out of a passionate concern for time,
the value, the urgency, the lack of time.

I need time, Lord, time to work a little harder,
earn a little extra, get ahead of the game.
I need time, Lord, time to spend at home,
live like a family, do things together.
I need time, Lord, time to get involved
in the struggles for justice, equality, and freedom for all.
What is this gift you give me, Father,
this time that runs through the fingers
like sand whenever I try to get a hold on it?
Yet sand can be beautiful, even bountiful,
handful after handful—sifting into the wind—
endless, timeless, eternal sand.

In this moment of calm, Lord, teach me
about time and sand.
Teach me about quality rather than quantity of time.
Help me to see that I do have time,
the minutes of every hour, the hours of all the days,
time—time enough—and more,
time filled up and running over.
Time to be, time to live, to love and serve.
Time to die—to die to self—to die for others.
Time, even, to begin to relinquish time,
to cling, not quite so desperately, to minute after minute.
Time to look at, to contemplate timelessness.

God, for time I thank you,
for the days and years of my life.
I offer them to you now, that of their minutes and hours
you may weave a richly hued eternity,
here and now, and forevermore.

DAY SIX

Being a Christian

Today, Lord Jesus,
I will be given the opportunity
to name myself a Christian once again,
to decide for you, or against you,
in every action, every word I speak,
every attitude I represent.
Today I will be called once more
to claim my citizenship in heaven, or in hell,
to exist under the authority of your love,
or under the tyranny
of my own protectiveness and pride.

Minute by minute,
hour by hour, I will know
the challenge to place my trust in you,
and you alone.
Each encounter, every decision,
even the most thoughtless
and incidental of acts will demonstrate
just who is really my Savior and Lord.
In every relationship,
at work, in school, on the street, on the road,
the choice will be there: to live your life for others,
or to live my own life for myself.

Be with me
in all of this day's moments, Father,
and grant me that gift
without which I cannot survive,
the gift of your gracious saving power,
working in me,
through me,
even despite me,
all things together for good.

DAY SIX

People

People throng my mind this evening, Father,
people with whom I have spent this day.

I recall those people I have hurt today,
by thoughtless action,
and by thoughtful, malicious, hot-tempered action.

I recall those people who have hurt me,
unintentionally at times.
and quite intentionally at other times.
And I ask you to permit me to share with them all
your gifts of forgiveness, reconciliation, and renewal.

I recall those people I have helped today,
in small everyday actions of kindness,
and in deeds of strong commitment.
I recall those people who have helped me
in all the myriad happenings, both large and small,
that have borne me through this day.
And I ask you to permit me to share with them all
your gift of thanksgiving and praise.

I call to memory also those people I have ignored today,
those whose essential contributions to my life
I have blindly accepted and taken for granted,
those who have shared the day with me
and whom I have not even noticed,
those who are so far away from me
that I have no conception of their existence,
their births, their joys, their griefs,
their celebrations and their deaths.
And I ask you to permit me to share with them all,
if nothing else, at least the sense of your presence,
and the power of your eternally overwhelming love.

Through Jesus Christ who was and is
your presence, and your love with us.

DAY SEVEN

Success

Lord, I will need
your support this day,
not only when I fail,
but also when I succeed.
For my successes
seem to set me even farther from you,
and from my fellow human beings.

When I fail,
I learn a lesson
in humility, if nothing else.
Failure makes me realize, even more,
my complete dependence upon you,
and upon other people.
But whenever I manage
to accomplish some great achievement,
I am on my own and proud of it,
dependent upon no one,
supreme master of my fate.

Lord, keep me
truly humble in whatever measure
of success this day may bring.
And grant, in all things,
whether failure or success,
that I might find you,
and finding you,
find all that I can ever ask,
or hope for.

So may
I live this day
in the fullness of eternity,
in the joy of your presence.

DAY SEVEN

Seeking and finding

I feel your presence now, Lord,
in the stillness of the evening,
and I am at peace—
like a tranquil pool, or a frost-bright winter sky,
a sunset city skyline, a bird rippling in song.

There is so much of peace around us, Father,
so much that is calm and patient,
so much of quiet, gentle loveliness.
A leaf caught in a breeze
flutters, yet is not frantic
as I have been this day.
A flock of pigeons scatters
from the sidewalk into sudden flight,
but soon settles back again, as if nothing had happened.
A woodland stream runs fast
across its rock-strewn bed,
but with none of the panic I have known.
There is violence and fear in nature,
but it seems brief, and swift in passing.
It does not disturb the overall symmetry,
the rightness of things, the fullness of peace.

Yet for me, Father,
and for so many of your human creatures,
the peace is what passes swiftly;
the panic, fear, and violence are what last.
And so our days are filled with the frenzied search
for what lies all around us, at our fingertips,
even behind our closing eyelids,
the tranquility of perfect trust in you.
Forgive my blindness to the subtle harmonies
of your world.
Let them feed me now,
and may I rest in peace this night.

DAY EIGHT

With me, Lord

Before I awaken this morning
you are with me, Lord,
and even as I open my eyes
you greet me with the gift of this new day.
May I take this certainty of your presence
with me into all this day can hold.

Be with me now as I go forth—
not as some weird
and ghostly watcher-over-me,
but as a deeper and truer awareness within:

an awareness
which is constantly
opening my mind to ideas,
to possibilities,
to relationships,
to understandings;

an awareness
which is constantly
opening my heart to trust,
to hope,
to sharing and giving,
to the call of the needs
of my fellow creatures;

an awareness
which is constantly
opening all of my senses
to the hidden joys,
the tiny discoveries,
the lesser celebrations
and the over-arching wonder
of your gift of life.

DAY EIGHT

Your mysteries

O Father, Son, and Holy Spirit,
although I have been taught
to speak and think of you as one God,
three in one, and one in three,
in fact you are a mystery
beyond all my thought and reason and understanding.
And for this I praise and glorify your name.
For I have learned that mystery is a quality
that pervades so much that is basic
to the richness of my living.

Who can explain
the chemistry of music and poetry,
laughter and liking,
that strange and secret power
that draws persons together,
and unites them in a glance,
a smile, even a lifetime?
My days are spent surrounded by the unknown,
and even our science can only describe,
but seldom, if ever, really explain
the heights and depths of our existence.

I thank you, Lord,
that even though you are beyond my grasp,
you are still within my reach,
that even though I cannot hold
and fully comprehend you,
you can and do touch me
and call me out into the greatest mystery of all,
the mystery of life in you.

So make this day, for me, a further exploration
into the inexhaustible mystery
of your presence and your promise.

DAY NINE

Listening

As I begin to pray this morning,
I am aware that I have far too much to say,
and far too little to listen for.
Catch hold of me in prayer, Lord.
So much of what I say
is simply a going-through-the-motions,
a speedy repetition of sacred phrases,
calculated to produce a warm,
if somewhat vacant, glow deep inside.

Break into my prattle, Lord.
Drive out the money changers
from the temple of your presence,
those bargain-basement prayers:
Father, make me pure—but not yet.
God, grant me success—then I will believe.
Lord, let me fall in love—and I'm all yours.

Interrupt my fevered chatter, Father.
Replace my empty noises with the fullness of your silence.
And in that silence let me hear
your simple word of truth that calls me into life.
The truth that I am yours, and not my own.
The truth that your faithfulness will never abandon me,
that even in the most painful and desperate moments
all of your love, all of your power
is on my side, forever.
The truth that there is work for me to do,
to share that love and power, to make it a reality,
not only in my life, but in the lives of those around me,
and especially those in need.

Let me hear, and know, and live your truth, Lord.
Then send me forth to do your holy will
in Jesus' name.

DAY NINE

Review

From all the random busyness
and scattered encounters
of this day that is ending—
from conversations and obligations,
impulses yielded to
and impulses suppressed,
acts of love, acts of hate, acts of emptiness,
from breakings and mendings,
laughings and cryings—
from all the richness and the barrenness
of these hours which are now past, Father,
I draw myself together into prayer.

As the moments of this day
pass before me in review, I become aware
of something sensed, at times,
yet never fully recognized:
your presence in all of my living,
speaking to me subtly
through the soft light of morning,
the occasional tones of music and song,
refreshing me in sunshine, and in coffee,
in smiles and handclasps,
calling to me through appointments,
news broadcasts, and meetings,
judging me in silences, moments of failure,
outbursts of anger,
forgiving me, accepting me,
supporting me,
rejoicing me in grace upon grace,
resting me in the purple shades of evening,
and restoring me now,
in this simple act of worship.

Thank you, Father.

DAY TEN

Manna

While they wandered
in the wilderness, Lord,
you fed your people, the children of Israel,
with the gift of manna from the skies,
bread falling from heaven—new every morning—
sufficient for the day,
and only for that day,
to be eaten in joy and thanksgiving
and never stored up for tomorrow.
And for those who doubted
and sought to hoard
your bread of life,
their store turned foul by morning.

Early in this morning, Father,
I rise to gather the fresh manna
of your love.
Fill me now to overflowing
with the strength, the grace, and the truth
I will need for the tasks ahead.
Then go with me
to ensure that
I give these gifts away,
that I spend them all
as currency for this day,
keeping nothing for myself,
guarding no store for the morrow,
sharing your gifts
in all that I do,
all that I am—
lest like manna of old,
stored love turns stale,
and poisons its possessor.

DAY TEN

Stretching

When I come to you in prayer, Father,
at the end of the day,
I come before you in confession,
not because this is the correct thing to do,
not because I know that I ought to feel guilty,
but because, as I look at myself and my life,
in the quiet and calm of this hour,
I begin to see myself as you must see me.
I begin to see how petty and trivial
my life has become, how small,
how crushingly small,
has been the content of my days.

You have granted me life, abundant life,
and I have chosen merely to exist.
You have given me people to love and be loved by,
and I have chosen to love myself, alone.
You have set me within a boundless creation,
and I have chosen to be bound by the limits
of my own narrow self-interest.

I have sold my birthright
for a mess of pottage, traded in
my priceless freedom for a solid investment
in security, and a reasonable, if modest prospect
of what is known as success.

Forgive me my smallness, Lord,
And in your forgiveness renew me.
Bestow, yet again, your eternal gift of new life,
so that grasping my newfound freedom, and living in it,
I can so broaden my narrow boundaries that they stretch
to include all of life, and all of humanity.
In this gift of life I rest the night.

DAY ELEVEN

In the world

Lord, I am preparing to enter a world
which can get along very well without you—
or so it believes.

In the situations, the assignments, the relationships
I will face during the next few hours,
the unspoken assumption will prevail
that you do not exist; or if you do exist,
that you are not concerned about such mundane matters
as make up my day.

Questions of morality, problems of justice,
the determining of your will,
the welfare of all humankind—
these are matters we would prefer to leave out
of our everyday affairs.
They make for interesting conversation,
but when they begin to complicate
that already overcomplex process of earning daily bread,
then we simply cut them out of our consideration.
"Life is hard enough as it is,"
we say—or words to that effect—
and we get on with business-as-usual.

Teach me, Father, how to be truly "in the world"
and yet not "of the world."
Show me once again, as you did in Jesus,
how I can love this world, celebrate its beauty,
even give myself to it in service,
without adopting all its ways,
its values, its assumptions, its priorities.

In all I do this day
let my vision be set
not by the boundaries of this world,
but by the horizons of your kingdom.

DAY ELEVEN

Those around me

There are so many who need my prayers, Father,
so many that, at times, I despair of praying.
Yet, I pray again tonight in the faith
that sets me actively to the answering of my own prayers
in your name.
In this faith, then, I dare to pray.

Tonight I remember especially
all those with whom I share my everyday life.
I pray for my family, at home, and far from home.
I pray for those who work with me,
those who direct my work,
and those who assist it, or complete it.
I call to mind and heart my friends,
and also those with whom I contend,
those who threaten me, and those whom I threaten.

Grant, Lord, to all of them,
and to me, the experience of your grace.
Persuade us, once again,
that whatever we do, or do not do, we are not judged,
we are not valued, nor are we loved,
solely on the basis of our achievements.
We are not justified by success, nor damned by failure.
But we are affirmed simply and completely as persons,
persons of infinite value,
persons bearing the potential and the privilege
of sharing with you in the greatest of all acts,
the acts of creative love,
of life in freedom and responsibility.

Lord, help me take this wisdom into my being,
into my attitudes, into all my living,
that I might rejoice in the fullness
of the brotherhood and sisterhood of all creation.

DAY TWELVE

First and last

Lord, let me live this day
as if it were my first day,
or my last.

Let me bring to it
all the wonder and amazement of a newborn child:
the trust
that welcomes everyone I meet,
expects of them only the best,
and grants them the benefit
of every possible doubt;
the openness
to catch the unsuspected beauties,
and unexpected opportunities of each hour;
the purity of soul
that places all its hope in you
and, thus, is infinitely optimistic.

But let me also bring
the wisdom and experience of the aged to this day:
the mellow ripeness
that can afford to rest a while,
and share a smile and a story;
the tenderness
that grows from years of care and gentle giving;
the hope
that has been forged through all the fires of doubt,
and even of despair,
and still, even better than before,
rings true and clear,
and points itself to you.

Lord, help me make this day
as fresh and new as a spring flower,
and as strong and secure as the eternal hills.

DAY TWELVE

Idle chatter

It is so easy, Father, to discuss the words of life,
to talk the talk of faith.
We stress the importance of dialogue,
yet we ignore the content of your dialogue:
"Whoever would be great among you,
let him be the servant of all."
We are enthusiastic over the need for communication,
yet we forget that the only way you could communicate
was by giving yourself completely.
We are eager to relate to one another,
yet we have not learned the basic lesson
of giving before we receive,
of losing life in order to find it.
We talk so freely of "love."
Yet we seldom, if ever, allow ourselves to realize
that love is no wishy-washy, doormat existence
that love can be a stern taskmaster,
that love can mean saying *No,*
can even mean alienating people,
causing pain, as well as feeling it,
that love is still the surest, fastest way to the cross.

Forgive me, Lord, this trivialization of ultimate truths.
Deliver me from my smooth sincerity,
my authorized authenticity,
my institutionalized integrity.
Set my feet on the long road
of working out what it means to truly love,
and serve, and be sincere.

May I have that mind in myself
which was in Christ Jesus,
who humbled himself, and became obedient unto death.
For in this is my integrity,
my dialogue, and my communication.

DAY THIRTEEN

Easing pressure

In the heat of this day, Lord,
may I know your cooling presence,
calming my tension, soothing my fears,
bringing into all the pettiness,
all the overwhelming detail,
all the mind-boggling complexity,
the perspective of your simple word of grace:
"Consider the lilies."

In the din and clash of the next few hours, Father,
let me hear your voice,
centering all relationships, all encounters,
all dispute and controversies,
in the challenge:
"Love your neighbor as yourself."

In the push and shove of my work, Lord,
let me feel your hand,
examining all my decisions,
all my dealings, all my hopes and fears,
in the eternal light of:
"Seek first the kingdom of God."

In the traffic jam of my brain, Father,
may I know your wisdom,
reordering all urgencies,
all priorities,
all dreams and ambitions,
under one supreme claim:
"I am the Lord, your God."

Thus may I walk
by the power of your word,
and not my own.

DAY THIRTEEN

Myself, yourself

This evening, Father, as on so many evenings,
I am concerned about myself.
I realize that self-concern can be dangerous.
But it persists. I am concerned about myself.

The heart of the problem is
my self just doesn't measure up.
I am not smart enough. I am not popular enough.
I work too hard, then I do not work at all.
Everyone seems to be better than I am at something.
And so, I guess, I am good for nothing.

Naturally I manage to fool some of the people—
some of the time,
maybe even most of the people—most of the time.
But deep inside there lurks the cold suspicion
that all I am, and all I do, is marked by failure.
And too often that suspicion becomes a certainty.
Lord, I have failed—I have failed.

Teach me again tonight, Father,
the lesson that Jesus taught, that Jesus lived,
the lesson of atonement.
Convince me once again that you have seen
all my failures,
and have covered them over,
blotted them out from your sight forever.

Help me to accept myself, as you have accepted me,
recognizing failure, fully admitting its reality,
yet beyond all failure, affirming my own ultimate value
as your child, created in your own holy image.
Grant me, Lord, the grace of self-acceptance.
And in that grace lead me to accept others also
as fellow heirs of your abundant, creative,
and redeeming love.

DAY FOURTEEN

Fool

Lord, there is in my nature
that which cannot bear
to be made a fool,
to feel like a fool.

Somehow I would rather
feel a cheat, a crook, a liar even,
than to feel a fool.
At least, then, I would have my wits about me.
But a fool is witless.
And at times I value my intelligence
even more than my integrity.

Show me, today,
the wisdom of your foolishness, Father.
Overthrow the wisdom of this world
from its dominion over my life.
And let my living
be determined by Jesus,
the crucified one.

Let this foolishness,
the foolishness of the cross,
the foolishness of radical openness,
the foolishness of self-sacrificial giving,
of losing life, and thus finding it—
let your foolishness be my wisdom this day, Father.

And thus, may I affirm with Saint Paul:
The foolishness of God
is wiser than men.

In the name of Jesus Christ I ask this,
who became a fool for my sake.

DAY FOURTEEN

Aging

Another evening, Lord, another day:
a day older,
but not necessarily richer, or wiser;
a day closer to the weekend, the vacation,
to a time when I can relax and rest a while;
a day closer to that day, whenever it be,
that will be, for me,
the last day, the day I die, the end.

Father, I am afraid even to think about that day,
its pain, its parting, its awful finality.
I love my days,
and so I live my days—most of them—
as if that day will never come,
as if, for me, there will be no end,
no closing of the book, no cutting of the cord.

Teach me, Lord, as I now prepare myself for sleep,
so to prepare myself for death.
Create in me a simple trust that morning will come,
that there will be awakening,
and greetings, and a great reunion,
breaking fast around your table.
Teach me again the poet's lesson
that parting is such sweet sorrow,
preparing, as it does, for an even sweeter reunion.

And grant me,
as a follower of the one who conquered death,
the steady and growing assurance
that in death, as in the finest moments of life,
I will be with you—
which is all I can know,
and all I can wish for.

DAY FIFTEEN

Escape

It is an amazing gift, Lord,
to begin the day in prayer,
to open the doors of the morning in your presence,
and in the knowledge of your blessing.

Yet, even as I pray,
I realize that prayer,
like all your gifts, can be abused.
Preserve me then, Father,
from that false use of prayer
which seeks to use you as an escape
from the trials and troubles of this world.

Let this, my time of worship,
be an hour in which the suffering of humankind
becomes more, and not less, real for me.

Grant me to share at least a little of your perspective
on the agony of your children,
my brothers and sisters.
Reveal to me the failure,
the inadequacy, of my vision,
which does not yet compel me
to see myself, and yourself,
in each and every victim of despair.
Permit me a glimpse
into the anguish of your heart,
that anguish which only Jesus fully knew
and shared upon the cross.

And, in the power of that cross,
deepen my compassion,
renew my dedication
to the way of the Lord Jesus Christ,
who came, not to be ministered unto,
but to minister,
and to be servant of all.

DAY FIFTEEN

Demand and invitation

My day has been swamped in demands, Lord,
laying their claims upon me, sinking their claws deep:
demands for food and shelter, for security and sympathy,
for artistic expression and sexual gratification,
for status and significance and hope.
Demands can be other people too, Lord:
demands of family and of friends,
demands of neighbors, fellow citizens,
fellow victims, fellow human beings.
Demands, demands, demands . . .

Yet among, and even within, the demands of today
there have also been the invitations,
of necessity quiet and low-key, but there, nonetheless:
a morning of crisp sunlight,
a book of poems, a piece of clay,
the smell of fresh coffee,
the sound of singing close at hand, laughter, tears,
arms outstretched, the eyes of a child.

The demands are real. I know that, Father,
and I cannot turn them off, though they din
till my head and my life spin in circles.
But I need your help to see, Lord,
that the invitations are real too—just as real,
just as essential as the demands.
And either one, without the other, destroys,
making of life a tormented, guilty hell on earth,
or an empty heaven, void of caring, of commitment,
of self-giving.

Continue, Lord, to set my days
within your divine context of demand and invitation.
And open my eyes to discover in this
life which is bountiful and abundant.

DAY SIXTEEN

Providence

Go into this day before me, Father,
just as your grace has always preceded me:
claiming me in baptism,
keeping me in childhood,
guiding me in adolescence,
preserving me until this moment,
preparing me
for the glorious daily privilege
of life in service
and in communion with you.

In times of stress and worry,
when the future seems a dark cloud,
and the lightning starts to flicker on the horizon,
when I begin to be afraid about my health,
my financial security,
the well-being of my family,
and those I love,
remind me again, Lord,
of how you have prepared a way
for me, and mine.

Help me to know
that wherever I am
you have been there before me,
opening the way.
And grant me the assurance
that somewhere up ahead
you wait for me,
with wonderful surprises in store.

This I ask in Jesus' name,
in whom is my future
with you.

DAY SIXTEEN

Testing

O God of truth,
of justice,
and of deep-searching, demanding love,
I thank you this morning that you put me to the test,
that you have, and still do, set before me
opportunities to stand
for what is right and good, pure and lovely,
that you beset me, behind and before,
with challenges and the call to high adventure
where the stakes are life and death.

Forgive me that most of the time
I am quite content to share
the immense wealth and power of this land
while your people still perish.
Forgive me that most of the time
I fail even to recognize the golden idols.
So well disguised are they—
success, comfort, security,
prestige, and gracious living—
that I worship them
without realizing that I am spending my life
flat on my face.

Make me aware again, Lord, of my idolatry,
those deep, often subconscious longings
that lord it over my life.
And then stand with me in the fiery furnace,
that when I am tested my dross might flare away
and your image in me remain pure and clear.

And grant me, Lord, no more than the privilege
of following in your footsteps,
through him who led the way for all,
Jesus, your Son, my Savior.

DAY SEVENTEEN

Incarnation

Two thousand years ago, in Palestine,
your Word took on our flesh,
was born a human child,
and lived, and died for us,
in Jesus.

But that was not the end.
Jesus arose from death
to live eternal victory
at your right hand—
and also, we believe,
to walk this earth again
in those who bear his name,
and try to live his life.

As I begin this day,
become flesh again
in me, Father.
Let your timeless and everlasting love
live out this sunrise to sunset
within the possibilities,
and the impossibilities,
of my own, very human life.

Help me to become
Christ to my neighbor,
food to the hungry,
health to the sick,
friend to the lonely,
freedom to the enslaved,
in all my daily living.

Thus may I know the life of love,
the presence of joy,
the hope of glory.

DAY SEVENTEEN

Opening

Lord, teach me to be open, and receptive in my praying.
So often, when I pray,
the only thing that is open is my mouth.
My eyes are shut tight,
and with them my mind and my heart.
Lord, teach me to be open to the leading of your Spirit
as I pray.

In these times of concern for dialogue between persons,
I have allowed my praying to degenerate
into a tedious monologue
in which I do all the talking
and you do all the listening.
Yet it is written:
"Be still, and know that I am God."
And again:
"In quietness and in trust shall be your strength."

So teach me, Father,
that prayer is both a matter of speaking,
and of silence.
Draw especially close now
as I set a few minutes aside
to wait in silence,
and listen expectantly for your Word:
your judgment on my sin,
your forgiveness in Jesus my Lord,
your response to my requests,
your call to my readiness.

Let me learn again, Lord,
the prayer of your servant Samuel:
"Speak, Lord, for your servant hears."
And let me make this prayer my own
tonight, and always.

DAY EIGHTEEN

Your family

People will be born today, Lord, and people will die.
People will marry, will leave home, will return again.
People will feast, will go hungry,
will make money, steal money, give money away.
People will succeed today, beyond their wildest dreams.
People will fail themselves into abysmal despair.
People will kill today, and people will love.

This human family, Father, is vast,
beyond all my comprehension,
beyond even my compassion.
I know it is here,
at times, I even admit to being a part of it,
but its complexity, its contrasts, as well as its sheer size,
overwhelm me.
Yet we are all your family, Lord.
Bring us closer together.
Help us to care for one another,
not only in an occasional prayer, like this one,
but in the way we spend our time and our money,
cast our votes, and raise our children.

In the way that I live this day,
may I demonstrate, at least respect,
if not outright love, for all human beings.
Renew in me, Lord, the realization
that the loss of any individual diminishes me,
for we all have something to share,
something to teach, something to give.
Thus let me make the human family
less an ideal, more a reality,
in my own life,
and in the life of my own small family.
In the name of Jesus, who first taught us
to call you, "Father."

DAY EIGHTEEN

ᴄᴏ

Security

So much of my living, Father,
is bound up in the search for security.
Desperately I seek after life without risks,
ironclad assurances, complete coverage,
guaranteed guarantees.

No sooner have we humans stepped into this world,
than we commence preparations
to cushion our departure:
retirement plans, pension schemes,
annuities, benefits, double indemnities,
precautions for a future which may never arrive.

Teach me, instead, to live with insecurity, Lord,
to realize that life is essentially insecure,
and to accept, and affirm it as such,
in all of its glorious insecurity.
Show me, again, that the grave
is totally secure—
no risks, no chances, no hopes.
Weave into the fabric of my daily life
the message of the parables of Jesus,
that we can secure nothing against death,
nothing except abundant life
in this present, eternal moment.
And in this message let me find all the security there is,
all the security I could ever hope for:
the secure assurance that, in this
and in every fully lived moment,
I stand in your presence,
I rest within your care,
I participate in love,
the only thing which is truly,
and eternally, secure.

DAY NINETEEN

Dreaming

Dreams, Father. What are they?
Where do they come from? Where do they go?
I awaken in a sweat of terror, or a glow of delight.
The alarm clock reprieves me at the last minute,
or deprives me of the final moment of fruition.
And I lie and wonder about dreams.

Sometimes it seems a whole lifetime is spent
in the passing of one brief hour of sleep.
At other times,
one moment of anguish, bewilderment, or bliss,
is all that is known before rising.
Sometimes I seem to be places I know,
with people I love.
At other times I do not even know
where or who I am.

One-third of my life is spent in dreams, Father,
and when I do not dream, I am not fully rested.
Are dreams, perhaps, my wishes
and my fears come to life in an inner world?
Or are they simply the result of something I ate,
a piece of cheese, or too many cups of tea?

Strangest, maybe, of all your gifts of life,
might it be that dreaming
prepares us for your closer presence,
reminds us that all that we are,
waking or sleeping,
is bounded by a vast and holy mystery,
the mystery and the majesty of your being?

For that mystery, I thank you,
and am content in knowing
that even in the depths of slumber
I rest within your everlasting arms.

DAY NINETEEN

Strength in weakness

Lord, there are weaknesses,
and then, there are weaknesses.
For, although I realize how weak I am,
I have a hard time discovering your strength
in my weakness.

I know very well what weakness is all about.
Time after time I have assented to your simple words:
"Save your life—and you will lose it.
Lose your life, for my sake—and you will find it."
Yet, time after time,
I have proceeded to behave exactly as I have always done:
saving my own life, protecting my own interests,
using people, rather than serving them,
living a life of manipulation,
of making deals, of easy compromises.
I talk about "love," read about, sing about "love,"
but love itself is conspicuous
only by its absence from my existence.
Yes, Lord, I know what weakness is all about.

Forgive me, Father,
for persisting in my own weakness.
Help me to find myself in your weakness:
that radical weakness before all the world holds strong,
that weakness in terms of success, strategy,
power, and prestige, which you can transform
into a deep and abiding strength,
that weakness we see in Jesus,
who in his living, and dying, and rising again,
showed us the true meaning of strength,
of the powerful acceptance of suffering,
of glorious victory through defeat,
of triumphant life through death.

DAY TWENTY

My mind

I thank you, Lord,
for all the wisdom of the past,
for the devoted labors of teachers and scholars
who have prized truth above all else,
for the discipline of clear, sharp thinking,
and the dissipation of confusion and prejudice.

Grant me grace, this day,
to continue in that passion for the truth.
Teach me to care
more for honesty
than for systems,
or for skill in debate.
And give me the patience
to keep open those questions
which cannot yet,
and perhaps never will, be answered.

Father, make me free
and alert in my reading and my thinking.
In the clear light of your truth
let me discern what value to set
on each one of this day's events,
and how best to deploy my resources
for today's decisions.

When I have to choose,
as so often I must,
between two evils,
give me, at least, the will to do the right,
and the assurance
that, even when I am at my wit's end,
I am never out of reach
of your mercy.

DAY TWENTY

For our riches

I pray today,
not only for the suffering,
the hungry, the war-torn, the lost,
for they are always in my prayers.
But I pray for the wealthy,
the prosperous, the comfortable of this world.

Open the sleepy eyes
of the wealthy nations, Lord.
Awaken us from our overfed slumber
to responsibility for our needy brothers and sisters.
Teach us, again,
how much we have that we do not need,
and how much they need that they do not have.
Persuade us,
set the conviction deep within us,
that our comfort is at their expense,
our well-being at the cost of their misery.

Set us free, Father,
from our clinging to the overstuffed life.
Set us free, Father,
for the bringing of life,
basic life, to all humankind.
Show us our task
in these days when the world
and its resources grow ever more limited:
never simply the preserving of a national way of life,
rather the provision for the first fully human way of life.

May my life, Lord,
begin to witness to these truths
and to follow the path of the one
who gave his life to save our lives
and to bring life, new life, to all.

DAY TWENTY-ONE

Abraham

O God,
you are calling me out
into a completely new day,
a day in which I will encounter
the unexpected, the strange, the unknown.

May I go forth, as Abraham did, long ago,
abandoning the clinging comforts of conformity,
rejecting the sham support and security
of all that is false and dishonest,
and trusting only in you,
your promises,
your presence to guide,
your power to preserve me from all evil.

When I am tested—
as I know I will be tested—
let me respond out of love,
the depth of your love in me.
May I be ready to give myself
even to the utmost,
for you, and your gospel,
and for those for whom you died.

And when I reach the end of this day,
draw me to yourself again,
and let my day have been to some
a source of blessing,
and to me a source of deeper faith.

In the name of him who was,
even before Abraham was,
Jesus Christ my call,
my guide,
my goal.

DAY TWENTY-ONE

Your day

This day, Lord, has been your day,
but I have sought to make it my own.

I have pulled it out of shape,
fractured its delicate framework,
and hopelessly entangled its contents,
in a vain attempt to use this day
rather than to live it.

Instead of allowing this day
to fill my life with living,
I have contrived to fill the day
with my own needs,
concerns, demands.
And so I have wasted the day,
torn it apart,
soiled its original freshness,
and now it lies shattered
all around me.

Pardon me, Father,
my willful disobedience,
my petty selfishness.
And in these quiet moments
let me salvage at least
the closing of this day for you.

Make this evening hour,
once again, your hour,
that, in yielding myself
to its contours and rhythms,
I might lose myself
and find myself
in the vastness
of your grace.

DAY TWENTY-TWO

Weather report

Each morning, as I awake, Lord,
I raise the blind to check the weather.

It makes such a difference to me,
this rain-or-shine world.
Perhaps it really shouldn't, but it does.
A sunny, crisp morning in January,
a cool, clear sunrise in May,
and I begin the day ahead of myself,
ready for anything—or almost anything.
But a frigid, drifting Monday,
or a damp and dreary Wednesday morning,
can end a day before it has even begun.
Of course, I realize, "We need the rain,"
and "Into each life a little rain must fall,"
but whenever it falls into mine,
it depresses me just the same.

Lord, teach me to praise you
for all states and conditions of life.
For, just as the rain brings nourishment and growth,
new strength to the earth, preparing it to blossom
with the return of the sun,
so times of trial and pain,
difficulty and hardship in my life, seem to be times
in which I sink my roots deeper and grow taller.

Help me this morning, whatever kind of morning it is,
to receive it as my morning, your-gift-to-me morning,
as yet another opportunity, rain or shine,
to spend some time with me, and with you.
Let your sun rise splendid in my heart now,
and send me forth to bear your radiance
to all I meet this day.

DAY TWENTY-TWO

Word power

From a world crammed full-to-overflowing with words,
I seek the peace and calm,
the evening quiet, of your presence, Lord.

For hour upon hour
words have tugged and taunted me,
delighting me, arousing me, seducing me, wearying me,
deluging me from printed page and lighted screen,
from radio, typewriter, and telephone.
Across the breakfast table they pour,
across the bench, across the classroom, across the counter,
swamping, submerging, drowning my brain.

What a wonderful thing it is, at last,
to be still and taste the silence.

In this time of peace, Father,
let me hold my peace, and listen for your Word.
Send forth the Word
to cut through the clamor and din of today's Babel,
to speak to me, gently but surely,
of judgment, forgiveness, and hope.
Let the Word that became flesh in Jesus
speak to me now of deep-running joy
in you.

Above all, Father,
lead me ever further into that union with you
in which all the words begin
to take on new meaning,
meaning rooted and grounded
in your one, supreme word,
the word, "Love."
Thus may my words draw closer to yours.
Thus may the Word
sing through all of my living.

DAY TWENTY-THREE

Conflict

Father, these days are filled with disagreement,
and the potential for dispute seems to be ever present.
This very day, at times,
my views may not coincide with my neighbor's,
my desires may be too close to my neighbor's,
my fatigue, my impatience,
may blind me to the presence of my neighbor.
Assist me, Lord, to deal with conflict situations.

May I never be afraid to differ,
honestly and respectfully, with a fellow human being.
But may I also never seek to differ,
purposely look for points of difference,
and provoke conflict where conflict need not exist.
Let me not attempt to preserve peace at all costs,
even at the cost of truth.
But let me not be so jealous for truth,
a truth about which none of us can be all that certain,
that I am constantly quarreling and squabbling,
making mountains out of molehills
rather than moving mountains through love.
Teach me the difference, Father,
between honest and open disagreement,
even over crucial issues,
and that bitter and divisive conflict
which sets persons against one another,
destroys all respect for the humanity of the opponent.

Let me become, more fully,
a citizen of the new creation, inaugurated by Jesus,
the new, liberated humanity,
in which all the dividing walls are gone forever,
in which all hostilities have ceased,
and your peace has begun its reign.
Let your peace reign in my life this day, Lord.

DAY TWENTY-THREE

Night people

As I turn now to the hours of rest, Father,
let me pause for a moment, and remember those
for whom rest is an unobtainable luxury.

I think of those who are ill,
whose drugged sleep brings little or no refreshment,
only the temporary absence of pain.
I recall those who watch over the sick, Lord,
who spend sleepless hours struggling to bring health
or hoping and praying to alleviate suffering.
Those who work at night
are in my thoughts this evening:
the parent holding down two jobs
to provide for a growing family;
the truck driver enduring long and lonely hours
for a dream of happiness way up ahead;
the airline pilot,
human lives continually in her all-too-human hands;
the nurse-by-night, housekeeper-by-day,
struggling to support an already broken home;
the bartender serving up sympathy
to the same old sad stories;
the police officer and firefighter,
under fire, underpaid, under increasing pressure
to betray the trust of an unappreciative society;
the thief, the pusher, and the prostitute,
seeking survival at any cost
in the human jungle we call the city.

Let your spirit be abroad while I sleep, Father,
bringing hope to the hopeless,
comfort to those in pain, trust to those in turmoil,
and the knowledge of your presence
to all who need you this night.

DAY TWENTY-FOUR

Blood

The blood of life
goes pulsing through my veins this morning, Lord.
I become aware of its unceasing flow
in the daybreak silence of this moment,
and I give thanks for the wonder of my body.

This blood which rivers through us
is an amazing substance to me, Father.
It is so precious, so irreplaceable.
We cannot manufacture blood.
We understand so little about its nature.
And yet we shed it so easily, thoughtlessly, cruelly.
Blood flows and cries for vengeance from the soil
today and every day.
Blood binds us all together as your children.
No matter what the color of our skin,
the shape of our features, the land of our birth,
we bleed in common fellowship, rich and red.
And, given certain careful preparations,
one's blood can serve and save another,
regardless of race or class, age or sex.

In fact, Lord, the blood of one
did serve and save us all,
regardless of race or class, age or sex,
or even of moral and religious standing.
For Jesus
and his gift of life
transfusing a new being
into my old and aching veins
I give you thanks again, this morning, Lord.
And I pray that his life blood
may also pulse its way
throughout my living this day.

DAY TWENTY-FOUR

Food

I have feasted this day, Lord,
eaten more than I needed to eat,
eaten just for the sake of eating,
for the pleasure of the taste
and the texture of food in my mouth.
Lord, I have eaten my fill, and more than my fill.
My body rebels at this abuse.
I grow fat, and sluggish, without energy or stamina.
No longer a temple of the spirit,
my body becomes a decaying memorial,
testimony to the destructive powers of excess.

I have feasted this day, Lord,
and others have starved.

The very scraps left on my plate
could have sustained life for a week
somewhere, somehow.
Do not permit me to forget this, Lord.
Do not permit me to forget the hunger, the starvation,
of my brothers and sisters
in other lands, other continents.
Pursue me with the specter
of the starving infant of humanity
until I begin to turn my life around,
until I begin to care about starvation,
until I begin to use the life, the health,
the strength that is in my body
to serve your children,
to bring all humanity to a seat at the table of your grace,
at the table you have spread
for all of us,
or for none of us.

So may I share the banquet feast of love.

DAY TWENTY-FIVE

Defense

This day is no sooner begun
than I am feverishly at work
seeking ways to protect, to cushion,
to ease my way through it.
Lord, I am a defensive, risk-hating creature.
Everything must be nailed down for me,
guaranteed in advance.

I seek love.
I yearn to receive the love of others.
Yet I will not take the risk of loving first,
of taking the initiative.
I demand an assured return on love,
or I will not make the investment.

I want to be needed.
I need to feel needed, depended upon by others.
Yet I am afraid to admit my own needs—
my desperate need for you, Father,
my need for my fellow human beings.
I seek to escape my own needs
by feeling essential to others.

I hate being alone.
I crave human fellowship, the company of friends.
Yet I cringe, even more, from being known.
I create a false self, wear it like a mask,
preferring loneliness to the sharing of my true self.

Deliver me this morning, Father,
from the tomb of my defenses.
Set me free from the fortress of my fears.
And lead me out into the glorious fullness
of life which is lived in the open.
Grant me to live, this day, in the freedom of eternity.

DAY TWENTY-FIVE

Strangers

My day has been punctuated
by strangers, Lord.
Both at work
and in relaxation,
strangers have brushed
against the fringes of my life
and then moved on.
How have I greeted these strangers, Lord?
What stranger self have I presented to them?

I think about the strangers in your life:
the three who journeyed from afar,
the one who came by night,
the woman at the well,
and the one wounded beside the road.

You gave yourself to strangers.
And once, at least,
you came yourself as stranger
to the two on the Emmaus road,
revealing just as much
as they were able to comprehend,
until, at last,
the gift of hospitality exchanged,
you were known to them
in the breaking of the bread.

So teach me to be open
to your presence in the stranger, Lord,
to keep an open door,
an open time and place,
an open life.

And let me be no stranger
to your presence and your love.

DAY TWENTY-SIX

The dance

Teach me to dance, Lord.
I find it so difficult, somehow.
Clapping with a song, moving feet gracefully,
giving myself up to a tune, a rhythm, a beat—
all this is so hard, so creakingly stiff for me.
I prefer the plodding, measured tread of everyday.

We humans seem to march
so much more readily than we dance.
Whole nations pace in step to one idea, one leader,
one common fear, or hatred, or ambition.
Teach us to dance instead—
to link hands, and arms with each other,
and run, and skip, and leap,
and swoop, and fall, and rise again,
rejoicing in the freedom of being,
and of being together, with you and in you.

I recall those whose dance is slow this morning,
because of pain, or loss, or hunger,
or being left to dance alone.
I pray for all in chains,
whether self-imposed, or shackled from without.
You, yourself, Lord Jesus, have known
fetters and imprisonment.
So be with them, and let them know your presence,
sharing their lostness, hopelessness, and fear.

And now, Lord, send me forth,
dancing forth to break the chains,
to shatter all that keeps us from ourselves
and from each other.
Let me share with all your gospel
of liberation, of deliverance to all captives,
of life, full and free, and flowing with the dance.

DAY TWENTY-SIX

Resting

There is a kind of rest
which I am seeking this evening, Father:
not so much a passive resting—
simply doing nothing at all—
rather an active rest.

The kind of resting that I know
when I see a great building
resting on deep and firm foundations,
or a family, or church, or community
resting on a basic and shared trust,
despite the day-to-day problems and crises.

The kind of resting that I feel
when I am at peace, yet participating,
in silence, yet profoundly in communication,
with you and with the world around me.

The kind of resting that I have
in the conviction that, at the heart of all I know,
and of all I do not know,
you are there,
and you are love.

In this time of evening rest,
guide me to recognize,
and to reaffirm those things
which are true, and good, and beautiful.
And let me rebuild my life on these firm foundations.
Grant me the refreshment of that holy resting
which is never the denial of responsible action,
but rather the necessary preparation for that action.
Then grant me rest, Father,
and send me out tomorrow, renewed
for responsible action in love
and for peace.

DAY TWENTY-SEVEN

Simple things

For the elemental simplicity of this morning hour,
sunrise, bird-song, cold clear water,
I praise and thank you, Lord.
Prayer, too, should be a simple gift,
yet I make it so difficult sometimes.

You have told me to come to you as a child to its father.
But I persist in approaching you
in a more official capacity:
as parent, householder and status-holder,
citizen, church member, officer in this-or-that,
as if these roles and titles
could protect me from your gaze,
from the searching power of your love.

Instead of admitting my sins,
and then honestly asking forgiveness,
I fret about my failures, analyzing them,
discussing them with myself,
permitting them to dominate my life in a double way—
first, as I commit them, and then,
in a perpetual orgy of regret, and unresolved guilt.
In my praying, as in so much of life,
I cannot see the forest for the trees.

Speak to me, now, your simple word
of forgiveness, of healing and restoration:
"Thus says the Lord: 'I have loved you
with an everlasting love, therefore I
have continued my faithfulness to you.'"
Lord, help me to take this assurance
into the day that lies before me.
In all I do, may I act as one who is free,
free to find myself, free to be myself,
free to give myself, as Jesus gave, to the utmost.

DAY TWENTY-SEVEN

Prodigals

This week, as every week,
I took out the garbage, Lord,
piled it high at the curb,
a silent memorial to the prodigality of seven days
in the life of one family.
So much wrapping, so much packaging,
so much to glitter, and glisten, and attract.
Even in this one day, now ended,
I have used and discarded so much,
and with so little thought—
so much waste, so many trees
and other precious living things
torn down and shredded into deadly refuse.

Forgive me, Father,
my careless squandering of your bounty.
Grant me a new reverence for your creation.
Show me how to use, only when necessary,
and only as much as is necessary,
to use responsibly,
aware of the needs of others,
and to use carefully,
replacing wherever possible
what has been taken away.

Above all, instill in me
a fundamental respect for all my fellow creatures,
my fellow passengers on our tiny spaceship, Earth.
Let me begin, in my own daily living,
to build your earthly kingdom of peace,
to fit my life more sensitively
into the cosmic harmony that you have ordained.
Thus may your kingdom come,
your will be done on Earth.

DAY TWENTY-EIGHT

Rebirth

I am being born again, Lord,
thrust out of the warm and comfortable womb
of my hard-won security,
thrust out into a brand-new day of challenges—
challenges to touch, to taste,
to smell and hear and see,
the world that is being born all around me,
challenges to grow with your world
as it unfolds within your purpose.

It can be a painful process,
this growing, Father.
The womb of yesterday was so much cozier,
so much easier to cope with,
so much more shaped to meet all my needs and desires.
Now I have to solve these problems for myself.
The old ways are no longer available to me.
The past is the past,
and you await me in the future.
New ways have to be found,
new ways for a new world,
new ways that require creativity,
and verve,
endurance, and trust in the future,
which is in your hands.

I am being born again, Lord.
Rebirth is a difficult, yet everyday, miracle—
the miracle of passing from yesterday into tomorrow,
the miracle of growth, of development, of life itself.
Help me, then, to accept
the changes of these days, to affirm them now,
and to step forward to the call of this new day
with joy.

DAY TWENTY-EIGHT

Judging

A complex and dangerous faculty
is judgment, Lord.
I know it, I use it, and often, I abuse it.
I go through life,
I have gone through this day,
busily forming judgments, weighing persons
in my own peculiar balances
and, for the most part, finding them wanting.

Thus far, it has taken me a lifetime
to begin to understand myself.
Yet I am eager to size up a fellow human being
in the twinkling of an eye,
and then pronounce eternal fate
in terms of my future relationship
to him, or to her.

Father, forgive my snap and facile judgments.
Pardon me the easy way
in which I condemn my sisters and brothers.
Deliver me from this habit
that cuts me off from so much of the human family.
And let me reserve this faculty of judgment
for ideas, attitudes, and actions,
and for my own ideas, attitudes, and actions
before all others.

Grant that I might judiciously use my time, my talents,
my creativity, health, and strength,
not in judging others
but in seeking to understand them more fully.
In the name of Jesus I ask this,
who refused to judge us,
and died instead, to save us.

DAY TWENTY-NINE

Children

I hear the sound of children in the morning, Father,
and I rejoice in the sweetness of your gifts.

For little children speak to me
when I take the time to listen to them.
Children seem to have a message all their own
to bring to me,
to bear to the heart of this, our age.
Given half a chance, these children trust.
And that is no mean feat in this world.

Openness is theirs,
to gaiety and mystery,
to fun as well as fear,
to the movement of a caterpillar
and the crashing terror of a thunderstorm.
Self-control is not one of their strong points.
Spontaneity and hope seem to come much easier.
They want things, that is true.
They can pester the life
out of a day, or out of an adult.
But their wants, when we heed them,
are somewhat more easily met
than the desires that drive adults to distraction.
A candy bar, a trinket,
a little attention and human fellowship
is all they really want, nothing more.
Small requests for such great rewards
in honest smiles, true-to-life embraces,
and the privilege of sharing simple gifts with friends.

Help me, for today,
to stop teaching, and preaching,
and to start learning from children, Father.

DAY TWENTY-NINE

Thanks

As I look back, Lord,
there is so much for which I am grateful
in the events of this day.

I thank you for the good times:
the closeness with friends,
joining in a laugh,
a meal, a task, a plan for the future;
the presence of my family,
living with me, daily,
the challenge and the blessing of true intimacy;
the things that worked out,
all the tasks I have been able to accomplish
and complete during the hours now past.

But I also look back
at some bad times, Father;
times when friends have turned out
to be just as human as I am,
and have let me down when I needed them;
times, too, when I have failed
by accepting less than the best,
less than the ultimate standard of your love
as the judge of all I say and do;
times when the intimacy of my family
has been less a blessing than a curse.

Forgive these bad times, Lord,
the little daily crucifixions that add weight
to the awful burden you bear.
And accept my gratitude for all of the good times.

And now I rest,
knowing that all of my times
are in your hand.

FOR SUNDAY

Our day

This day is your day, Lord,
even more than all the others.

A day of rest for most,
a day of play for many,
a day for traveling and visiting,
for gardening and pottering,
for reading and thinking,
and writing,
and talking.

A day, for some, of praying
and singing,
confessing and hoping,
dreaming and planning,
living
in giving.

This day is your day, Lord.
Share this day with me, Father.
Let it also be my day,
sun-rising-upon-me day,
as well as your Son's rising day.

May I explore, today,
the depths of re-creation,
forming myself,
and my life anew,
in your eternal image,
and through your graceful, saving love.

So let this day
be our day, Lord.
And may its stream run fresh
through all the days of my years.

FOR SUNDAY

Worship now

Lord, worship is a strange activity
in this, the twenty-first century.
We know, only too well,
how to analyze and criticize,
to rationalize, and finalize.
The secrets of production and consumption,
of automation, cybernation, and organization,
are hidden from us no longer.
We can replace the human heart,
and set human feet upon the moon.
There is nothing we cannot harness and control,
except, it seems, ourselves.

So we come before you in worship:
a people all-sufficient,
yet strangely lacking,
a race infinitely powerful,
yet powerless to achieve true justice,
or peace, or truth.

Teach me the lesson
of this day that is ending, Lord.
Teach me to worship,
to know your presence,
to seek your forgiveness,
to become open to your power,
that power which is made perfect in weakness.
And in your power,
the power of love,
may I discover justice and peace,
and truth, and life.
Through him who was, and is,
the way,
the truth,
and the life.